T0198491

THE POWER OF
PERSISTENCE

The Struggle is Real

ALSTRIA COMPTON

authorHOUSE®

AuthorHouse™
1663 Liberty Drive
Bloomington, IN 47403
www.authorhouse.com
Phone: 833-262-8899

Published by AuthorHouse 03/15/2021

ISBN: 978-1-6655-2002-7 (sc)
ISBN: 978-1-6655-2003-4 (hc)
ISBN: 978-1-6655-2001-0 (e)

Library of Congress Control Number: 2021905450

Print information available on the last page.

Unless otherwise indicated, all scripture quotations are from The Holy Bible, English Standard Version® (ESV®). Copyright ©2001 by Crossway Bibles, a division of Good News Publishers. Used by permission. All rights reserved.

Scripture quotations marked KJV are from the Holy Bible, King James Version (Authorized Version). First published in 1611. Quoted from the KJV Classic Reference Bible, Copyright © 1983 by The Zondervan Corporation.

Scripture quotations marked NKJV are taken from the New King James Version. Copyright © 1982 by Thomas Nelson, Inc. Used by permission. All rights reserved.

This book is printed on acid-free paper.

I dedicate this book and my success in life to my grandmother Irma Jean Compton. Her relentless will has inspired me for as long as I can remember. Thank you for always being my angel. I love and miss you to heaven and beyond.

Proverbs 29:18 (KJV)

"Where *there is* no vision, the people perish: but he that keepeth the law, happy *is* he."

Contents

Acknowledgments

I'd like to thank:

- Jesus Christ, for blessing me throughout my life, including all the hard times, and always bringing me out on top; providing the insight and ability to write this book to help others; and continuing to bless each and every person who comes in contact with this book.

- My grandmother Irma Jean Compton for always being positive, even when we were homeless and told she only had a short time to live, and showing me what love is and how persistence can get me further every day by not sitting around doing nothing. She was always putting others' needs above her own. And finally she taught me to never cry in front of others.

- My mom, Charlene Compton, for all the beatings for stuff I did and didn't do that scared me enough to not do it. She made me a responsible man and helped me understand that forgiving is not about others but ourselves. She was teaching me that making a positive impact on the world is important and I was to always put God first.

- Allen James Compton (AKA Alstria Jayden James Compton), my son, for saving my life and making me realize the true meaning of 1 Corinthians 13:11 (KJV). "When I was a child, I spake as a child, I understood as a child, I thought as a child: but when I became a man, I put away childish things." Most importantly, he showed me what my why is. Because of him, I now know how to love beyond myself.

- My aunt, Dameron Compton, for always being my other mother (AKA my day-one supporter). She always had my back and supported me when I felt like the world was against me. She was teaching me life lessons and being that confidant.

- My Uncle Heath, who taught me how a man provides for his family and must take care of the women, as most of my family were women. He taught me what sacrifice is and how to always laugh. "Don't sweat the small stuff!"

I'd also like to thank so many others who provided support to me when times got hard or I just needed an ear to listen.

Each one of these individuals listed always gave me honest assessments and positivity to go on to continue my goals: Ricardo Bustos, Billy Jones, Angel Johnson, Gene Meredith, Christopher Bentley, Austin Olooaringo, Blake Keil, James Plat, Lisa Harriet, Michael, Patricia Meza, Manny Barnes, and Travis Fowler.

Foreword

What are your short- and long-term goals? What are you doing every day to get one step closer to your goals? No one has ever asked me these two questions, two inquiries I had never deeply considered. Sure, I had several short-term goals and very vague long-term goals like "I want to be successful," but who knew they required daily steps?

Alstria Compton asked me these two questions within two weeks of meeting me. These two inquiries have stuck with me as I navigate life.

Alstria was not born with a silver spoon in his mouth, yet he has managed to pull himself out of poverty, despair, financial hardship, a bitter divorce, and dangerous wartime conditions and become a better man, friend, mentor, and human. I believe the key to his success is his persistence to answer these questions and consistently revamp his goals. He carries a planner around and plans his life down to the hour because his goals are important to him; they represent his heart's desire.

What better person to learn about persistence from than a man with a plan and vision to see those plans through.

Many of us want to be successful at something. We want to find that something that unlocks all the potential locked up inside of us, and if you are reading this book, I can bet you are one of those people. So before you go any further in this book, I want you to ask yourself, "What is success to me? When I look back on my life at age seventy-five, will I think I lived a successful life, and what will be that deciding factor that determined my success?"

I know this sounds so much like those tough, annoying philosophical questions that Alstria asked me before. Like many people would have, I thought Alstria was absolutely crazy when he asked me those two questions. Like many would have, I also thought Alstria was asking for too much when he asked me if I planned out my days, weeks, or even months.

I am sure my response was along the lines of, "No! I'm just trying to survive this day, let alone plan for the next day! Goals? Goals? My goal is to make it through this day in Afghanistan and go to sleep. I'll think about being successful some other time. Maybe I'll win the lottery."

Although Alstria and I remained friends, it would be more than a year later, thanks to his mentorship and guidance, that I finally sat down and wrote out my short- and long-term (which are so hard) goals and started to use a planner to create some semblance of organization and productivity in my life. Honestly, it was not easy for me to think far in the future, and it was a little frightening to actually picture what I wanted my life to be like when I grow up.

It may not be easy for you, but I can tell you from experience that it is worth it. It will take you from feeling like a plastic bag blowing in the wind to feeling grounded and growing like a flower ready to bloom. Without Alstria's mentorship and guidance, I would not be the owner of an activewear business that has more than a half-million dollars in sales. I would be another twentysomething-year-old, not knowing what to do and just waiting for life to happen to me instead of me making life happen.

The Power of Persistence was inspired by Alstria's grandmother Irma Jean Compton, who overcame homelessness and illness to provide for her family and ensure they did not have to navigate the trials and tribulations of earth alone.

That inspiration probably resonates with a lot of us. We may have experienced having to navigate through poverty or witnessing a family member become ill while still trying to be our best selves. This book will provide you with a blueprint for unlocking your best you, not despite your struggles, but because of how your struggles have enabled you to unlock something deep down within your heart and soul.

Within these pages are some hidden and unhidden secrets to joy and reaching a state of euphoria. To reach greatness, we often must go through some trials and tribulations, and the journey often requires more than we think we can give and more than we think we can achieve. As Alstria says to me all the time, "We must stay focused and be persistent to accomplish our goals, no matter how hard it gets and no matter how frustrated we feel."

The Power of Persistence will take you on a journey from determining your heart's desire, something many of us have not considered, to discovering what persistence and sacrifice are, how success might look for us, and how we can attract success in our lives. You may be hesitant to take this journey, but trust me, you have already started the process toward success by picking up this book and making it this far. Let me be your friend for a moment and say "You can do this!**"**

Alstria does not try to use fancy words or catchphrases to sell you on something. He uses relatable examples from the Bible, his personal life, examples from others he has mentored, and exercises to provide you with tangible ways you can start on the road to success right now. Some of you may want to read this book straight through, but I encourage you to use it as an interactive tool and complete the exercises at the end of each chapter before moving ahead, even if you need to take a few days or weeks to truly complete the exercises. These exercises enable you to get a true and powerful self-assessment and realize how self-assessment can be the gateway of what you determine success to be.

If you are looking for confirmation that you picked up the right book, here it is! You can do this, and you can be successful! Let's start this journey. By Angel Johnson

Chapter 1

YOUR HEART'S DESIRE

Vision is the ability to think about or plan the future with imagination or wisdom. The first step is to determine what your vision is and whether it is your heart-desired vision. Looking into the future is amazing and has benefits that are unbelievable until seen in hindsight. From the time we were young children, we have been taught that we can do it: we should chase our dreams and plan for the future.

When I was in elementary school, we had a day set aside as career day, asking us children what we wanted to be when we grew up. The answer may be simple but complex to carry out. People can be anything they want to be if they follow the seventeen principles outlined in Napoleon Hill's book, *Think and*

Grow Rich, starting with "definiteness of purpose." Therefore, before starting, the true question that must be answered is, "What do you want to be more than anything else?"

This is your heart's desire. To define a heart's desire, we must dissect vision and identify how it is powered. This chapter will focus on true vision, a heart's desire, to convey an interactive logical process. According to *Collins Dictionary*, if you say that someone or something is your heart's desire, you mean that you want that person or thing very much. The Bible says to speak those things as if they will be and not as they currently are, in layperson's terms.

The following are seven of the most powerful verses from the Bible of speaking things into existence, my favorite being the second.

1. "Death and life are in the power of the tongue: and they that love it shall eat the fruit thereof." (Proverbs 18:21 KJV)

2. "Whatever things are true, whatever things are noble, whatever things are just, whatever things are pure, whatever things are lovely, whatever things are of good report, if there is any virtue and if there is anything praiseworthy— meditate on these things." (Philippians 4:8 KJV)

3. "And whatever you ask in prayer, you will receive, if you have faith." (Matthew 21:22 NIV)

4. "So shall my word be that goes out from my mouth; it shall not return to me empty, but it shall accomplish that which I purpose, and shall succeed in the thing for which I sent it." (Isaiah 55:11 KJV)

5. "Truly, I say to you, whoever says to this mountain, 'Be taken up and thrown into the sea,' and does not doubt in his heart, but believes that what he says will come to pass, it will be done for him." (Mark 11:23 NIV)

6. "But he answered, 'It is written, 'Man shall not live by bread alone, but by every word that comes from the mouth of God.'" (Matthew 4:4 KJV)

7. "Where there is no vision, the people perish: but he that keepeth the law, happy is he." (Proverbs 29:18 KJV)

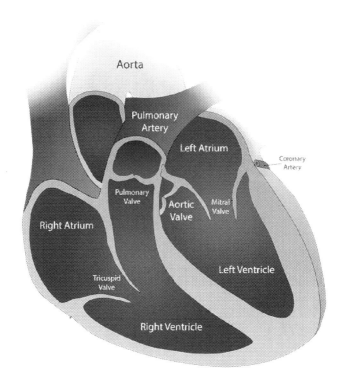

What is your heart's desire? It's not just a simple want by any means! Let me take you outside the box from which you see the world. What is the purpose of the human heart? Is it a function of the biological system, or is it a place where our deepest emotions ignite and grow? The answer is both!

Physically, the heart pumps blood to the body, giving us the ability to live our everyday lives in good or bad health. It transports all of the macro- and micronutrients that a living organism needs to function. We all have our own individual heartbeats, just as each of us has our own visions, dreams, goals, and wishes. Each snowflake is made of frozen water but differs in shape, and so too do our visions and goals.

We have to use and trust that our heart will do what it is designed to do. We don't trust that someone else's heart will pump the blood for us (unless it is a transplant). We must understand how our hearts work and why. This awareness will help facilitate a long and healthy life and prevent many illnesses.

The emotional heart works in the same fashion as the physical. When people become emotionally involved, they have a stronger attachment. This attachment has many names, such as love, hope, hate, and obsession.

Love! Whether it's learned or innate has been debated for generations. Either way, love creates a bond that is not easily broken. Do you remember Linus from *Peanuts*? He dragged a blanket around with him everywhere he went. You didn't see one without the other. It would be fair to say he loved that blanket, right?

So what do you love? What or who has your heart? When we love with the emotional heart, it is necessary to pump life into that thing. Let's call it your why. What do I mean? First, understand what our why needs to survive and thrive, the micro- and macronutrients that give it life. This is how dreams become reality, by first becoming self-aware and understanding the environment around us.

So what are these micro- and macronutrients? That is a complex question. Having a healthy physical diet consists simply of eating certain things that provide necessary nutrients and in the proper proportion of proteins, fibers, carbohydrates, fat, and so on. Essentially it depends on each individual and their fitness goal. Some emotional nutrients might be self-motivation, meditation, positive thinking, and reflection. All these things keep you focused on obtaining that goal of a healthy body or your dream. So recognize how you work! Is the way you work productive or counterproductive to your desired end state?

I speak specifically of the heart in this chapter to build a correlation to life as well as to emphasize how one has to desire physical and emotional goals with the heart—your unique lifeline. Throughout history, people's strong emotions, their heart, have changed the world. Think about Martin Luther King Jr., Gandhi, the Buddha, Michael Jordan, Walt Disney, Henry Ford, Oprah Winfrey, Barack Obama, Christians, Muslims, and so on.

Decide upfront: where is your heart? Not physically but emotionally. What are your dreams? Are they truly your heart's desire, or do you just want them? Will you die if you do not attain your goal? When the answer is yes, then you have your golden ticket, and it is time to map out your plan.

Heart disease has plagued the world for ages. In 2017 and 2018, several people died from heart disease. I am willing to bet that is still a hundred times less than the number of visions that die from mental and emotional heart disease. Heart disease or cardiovascular disease (CVD) is on the rise. This is evident in the amount of obesity displayed daily. There's nothing wrong with having some size, but ensure it is a size your heart can handle in good health.

From 1950 to the present, health consciousness has regressed. This is also true in dreams. When I was young, I often saw people working out with home videos, lifting weights, running, or walking. This helped stimulate the world by providing healthier people and generating better ideas.

I am writing this book on a computer in a combat zone. We have come a long way technologically, but we have to get back to basics when it comes to fitness. The CVD plague prompted me to create Fitness RoadMap to help others gain and maintain a healthy heart. I am no Eric Thomas or Tony Robbins, but I try to push positivity to anyone and everyone I can to stimulate their emotional heart. Unfortunately we have become lazy. When was the last time you didn't just think about it but worked out? Better yet, when was the last time you followed your heart in regards to dreaming? Don't be surprised if it were when you were a child.

Children are fearless. That's why they succeed. When they fall, they don't quit. They get up and try again or reformulate a plan of attack and try again later. But they don't quit until they accomplish their desired outcome, regardless of what it is—learning to walk, doing a flip, riding a bike, or driving a car. Maybe fear is a learned trait.

I recall as a child falling out of trees, jumping ramps on my bike, and even telling a girl I liked her. Neither rejection nor failure stopped or deterred me from climbing, riding, or trying to get my crush's attention. Wow, what happened to that stud? What happened to that fearless child in you? What are you doing with the power you have in you?

We have heart attacks, both physically and emotionally. There are four types of physical and emotional CVDs. The four main cardiovascular diseases that cause heart attacks are coronary artery disease (CAD), heart arrhythmia, heart failure, and heart valve disease.

Coronary Artery Disease (CAD)

CAD is a disease in which a blockage in your coronary arteries results in the decrease of blood flow into your heart muscle and consequent lack of oxygen. In the same way, the negativity of others can block your vision: "That's impossible," "That will never work," "You should have more realistic goals," and other blocking statements you may have heard. You know the saying "birds of a feather flock together"? Is this true? Do they? What do you think?

The truth is that attitude is infectious. As natural selection forces people and things to conform to the environment, so too do your emotions unwillingly absorb and reproduce those of the people you are around the most. If you allow negative people, thoughts, doubts, fears, or anything not aligned with your overarching vision, it will block your passage of blood flow, or positive reinforcement in the emotional sense. Your vision will soon have a CAD and die!

Increase your blood flow by understanding your vision and tying a date of achievement to it. Make it a goal! Continuously do things to facilitate a healthy process and progress until your heart's desire becomes a reality. This includes being selective of who you surround yourself with and take advice from. A few examples who have made an impact on everyone reading or listening to this book are some of the most renowned inventors, writers, and actors in the world.

Thomas Edison's teacher told him that he was too stupid to learn anything. I guess that was the light bulb he needed. This is the emotional plaque buildup that causes dreams to die, if you let it. Edison went on to be granted more than a thousand patents. Maybe lightning does strike in the same place twice or, in his case, a thousand times. What if he took ownership of his teacher's belief in him? The negativity of others is the number-one cause of death of dreams, or causation-emotional CAD.

Another example of CAD at work is Colonel Sanders, the chicken icon himself. He had a great recipe but was going broke. He decided to drive across the country and promote his product. During this time, he slept in his car many nights, but he had a dream and persistence. Doubt could have sat in, doubled, and continued to germinate for many people, effectively killing the dream. The constant negativity would have become so overwhelming that the positivity (blood) would not have been able to get to the heart, resulting in CAD.

So it is highly important that we guard our thoughts. When I was little, my mother would say, "An idle mind is the devil's workshop." Where is your mind, and is it productive toward your heart's desire? Only you can prevent forest fires, and only you can prevent CAD, both physically and emotionally!

Heart Arrhythmias

Heart arrhythmias are an irregular beat pattern. It can stem from previous CVDs but can also be its own issue. When it comes to our heart's desire, if we cannot find a normal beat in a positive direction, we will go nowhere fast. In other words, we will be dead in our tracks.

It is a must to gain a lot of small victories in pursuit of our vision. This keeps us motivated and our dreams alive. A disruption of our rhythm can have a ripple effect. This means our heart will not get blood and oxygen (physical) or positive reinforcement/ motivation (emotional) needed to live our best lives. You are the only one who can control your rhythm, and that includes what affects it. People, situations, and mostly doubt are the top hinderers of our heart's desires, resulting in heart arrhythmias.

Find your heart's desire and create a heartbeat like that of the Tasmanian people, known for having the healthiest hearts in the world. An example of this CVD occurred when I was young. I wanted to run in the Olympics, more so after going to the Junior Olympics in 1998. However, I came from a poor family, and as I got older, life happened. I had to work just to keep my head above water.

I joined the U.S. Army. I was faster than just about anyone I ran with, but in 2014 I ruptured my patella tendon to the point where my kneecap was in my thigh. I had surgery and went through physical therapy for eight months. Then the physical therapist realized that my kneecap was two centimeters too high, which caused more damage than expected.

After getting surgery for the third time, I was told I would never run again. This broke my spirit and increased the depression I already suffered from due to an unfaithful girlfriend. Before all of this, my life was great. I was the ideal soldier and overall positive human being. As I lay in that bed, the depression caused a bacterium to spread through my leg. The hospital staff could not figure out the cause. I knew what it was, but I was too embarrassed to say until the doctor walked into the room and told me that I had an infection in my leg and they didn't know what it was. He then reported that they had given me the strongest antibiotic allowed.

The last resort was to amputate my leg; else it would move to my torso, and I would die. This was an eye-opener! I told the doctor not to cut off my leg. He walked out of the room. I laid back and thought I only had a few hours to live and no one had called except for my ex-girlfriend's mother. Then it happened.

"Carpe diem!"

I heard it loud and clear. If I am going to die, why spend it stressing? Seize the day! At that moment, all my stress disappeared. I felt more alive than I ever did. The positive energy that surged through my body cleared my heart arrhythmias, and I was back on track. Ain't God good? This is what you say all the time!

As you can see, that small disruption had the potential to end my life, both physically and emotionally. Fortunately that positivity, or blood flow, was able to get through and reach my heart, both physically and emotionally.

Heart Failure

The third CVD is heart failure. "Well, aren't they all heart failure?" you may ask. That would be a no. Heart failure will constitute that the heart doesn't pump blood to keep up with its workload, but CAD normally causes it.

This is simple, people! If your heart doesn't pump blood, you die. So if you're not facilitating a productive, positive, motivational process to pump life into your heart's desire, your vision is dead. Don't die! Live your best life! Have you ever had a great idea and told someone? And then that someone told you not to waste your time, energy, or money on that, just to see your idea make bank for someone else later in life. Doesn't that piss you off?

Many artists, including Hitler, fall into this category. What if Hitler's dream of becoming an artist didn't die due to others telling him his work was no good? Would he have become so evil? There is no cure for heart failure because once your heart reaches this point, it has probably endured enlargement, muscle mass, and/or faster-than-normal pumping. Your goals can also suffer from emotional heart failure. When you are constantly absorbing the negative thoughts, ideas, and affirmations about your dreams, visions, and goals, these will die in the same instance as heart failure.

Don't let others' opinions, fears, and doubts become your own. Be your own unique person. You are not like anyone else who has ever graced this earth. There has been, is, and will ever be one you. Be the best you and allow your heart to provide the blood and nutrients to the body, physically and emotionally, needed to thrive and conquer this thing called life.

One example of this is the elephant. This beautiful creature has been used for hundreds of years to build and destroy things, for example, buildings, forests, and more. But what keeps these animals from destroying carnival tents, zoos, or villages in some areas? The answer: a stake and rope!

That's right! Something that could be easily pulled from the ground without even trying. However, the elephant has been subject to the negativity of these items as a youth, resulting in them taking ownership of the belief that the stake and rope are immovable. This has, in turn, denied the elephant's freedom of movement, or heart failure. Their minds no longer think for themselves and become a victim of classical conditioning.

Heart Valve Disease

Heart valve disease is the opening and closing of the four valves to the four chambers and vessels. Disruption in the opening, closing, or any defect can result in improper blood flow, blockages, and/or leaks. Why do you think it's important to allow your motivation, positivity, and productiveness to flow systematically to achieve our heart's desired vision? Would negativity or lack of motivation ensure our vision comes alive? Is it important to have a balance in life, which includes our dreams?

Not getting fixed on one aspect of vision allows a process of having positive people, thoughts, and ideas to create motivation and opportunities for tangible and intangible vision achievement. Have you ever been going through something and you try to stay positive, but at your high point, you seem to get overwhelmed with negative thoughts? They could stem from a thought, email, sight, voice, memory, or someone else entirely. This is the heart valve disease acting on your emotional state.

Luckily there is a cure! I recommend building your mastermind group and daily positive support channel. Whenever you may feel like things are going south, call on your mastermind group for a recharge. The book of Proverbs seems to also assist me.

Story 1

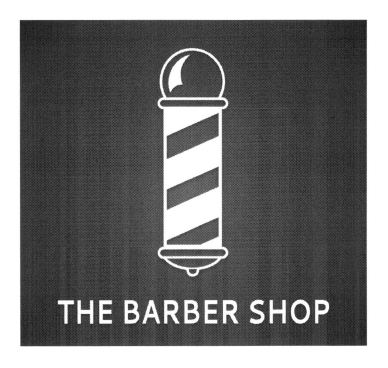

I have a friend, Stacey, who lives in Texas. He grew up in the projects of Chicago, where he got mixed up with gangs, as most poverty-stricken African-American young men do. When we first met, he was just opening a barbershop with another man. I was new to Texas, and as most black men with hair, I didn't want my hairline pushed back. So I contacted my barber, DJ from Oklahoma, and asked if he had any recommendations for barbers. He told me to use social media to look at top barbers and view some of their work. This led me to Stacey Styles of Texas.

Stacey once did prison time and realized his life wasn't where he imagined it as a child. He had a vision of being the most successful barber in Texas with multiple shops and a commendable brand.

One of the first conversations we had was about barbershops not being open on Sundays and the hours they are open. I saw then that I struck a nerve, and his mind was formulating a plan to fill that gap in the area. A few weeks later, he changed the hours and appointments. Now his business picked up quickly. He hired more barbers and beauticians. Soon he sold his products at the shop. Stacey is a pro bodybuilder, so he values his time, with it being divided into several parts such as family, gym, work, and social life.

As he began to build his brand and get more and more customers, he enhanced the shop with TVs, an ATM, new chairs and lights, a barber pole, and even floor tiles. I moved from Texas in May 2017. In June of that year, Stacey was the owner of two barbershops and a gym and had been selected to be an instructor at the barber college in Texas. Not bad for a poor kid from the ghetto!

When we talk about having a vision and a heart's desire, it is only fair to speak of Joseph. Many people might know him as a dreamer or prophet because he was able to see into the future. His first dream was introduced in Genesis 37, when he dreamed that his family would bow down to him. As he was the youngest, his siblings became enraged and did the unthinkable to him: they sold him into slavery with thoughts of this dream never coming true.

After being imprisoned, he would surely suffer with unstable mind and body effects, which his brother would put an end to his dream and lead to his demise. Ironically, unlike most people, he was not going to accept the environmental factors or let naysayers stop what God had shown him.

As we can only imagine the life of a slave during biblical times, he ended up in Egypt and ultimately became king, another satisfied customer in the store of vision and self-fulfilled prophecy. Joseph had unlimited opportunities to accept the negativity and die, both physically and emotionally. This would have been a sure CVD leading to heart failure, but as my mother says, "What God has for you will be yours!" What's your story?

8. As you can see, Stacey had a distinct vision and desired it with his heart. Once he saw his end state, he easily jumped into action. This proved to be a self-fulfilled prophecy of what he stated he wanted when we first met. The Bible says, ""Truly, I say to you, whoever says to this mountain, 'Be taken up and thrown into the sea,' and does not doubt in his heart, but believes that what he says will come to pass, it will be done for him." (Mark 11:23 NIV)

Stacey could have suffered from a CVD, being an African American from poverty, which most have a negative light of being dead by eighteen, and having a criminal background. Can you imagine the things he was told when he told others his dreams? Better yet, what do you think the banks might have said when he applied for a loan? Stacey's circumstances had the potential to cause him to suffer from all four CVDs, but he found his why, his family, which provided him enough positivity that it towered over his fears, doubts, and anything else that was going to stand in the way.

Michael Jordan said all he had to do was believe in what he saw and he could achieve it. Now you can see where he is! Do you see a pattern in all these instances? You must know where you truly want to go before you find yourself running around like a chicken with his head cut off! Your heart's desire is that distinct destination.

Exercise

If you are having trouble seeing where you truly want to be, try this exercise, which I got from Dean Graziosi: Millionaire Success Habits.

1. Ask yourself: why do I do what I do every day?

2. Now ask yourself why to the previous answer. Repeat six additional times. Your outcome will be your true reason why.

3. Now that you know your reason why, ask yourself: what do I like doing that is in line with my reason why and provides that facilitation for my operational definition of success?

4. Write it down, using as many details as possible.

5. Read it often—morning, noon, and night—for twenty-one days.

Now go figure out what you want out of life because we truly do have the whole world in our hands. The next chapter will help us understand how to navigate through the world's storms and into a state of euphoria.

Chapter 2

PERSISTENCE
(FUCK IT)

This chapter will illuminate what persistence is, when we want to embrace it, why it is important to encounter and press through the trials and tribulations that life throws at us, and what this says about you.

Persistence is defined as the fact of continuing in an opinion or course of action in spite of difficulty or opposition (dictionary. com). Simply put, "When the going gets tough, the tough get going." Another saying is "no pain, no gain." What do either the definitions or quotes mean to you? If there were a quote about how persistent you are, what would it say?

"Fuck it" is an expression used to convey a person's feeling of being fed up or not caring anymore. This can be both positive and negative. For example, if a person is so analytical that they avoid having fun because of the possible risk factor, then "fuck it" can help or hinder them. It can help by allowing them to experience life outside the bubble they live in. It can also cause a person to hurt themselves if not properly governed.

In the military, most people are taught to present the 5Ws: who, what, when, where, and why. This technique has been proven invaluable in getting through difficult situations—war, negotiations, leader and soldier development, strategic effects across the world, and many others. Please do not prejudge!

Just take a moment and think back in your life whether it was business, relationship, educational, economic, social, family, or some other time you were faced with an opposing force! Would knowing the 5Ws have helped you develop and execute a plan to get you through those times? I'm willing to bet your answer is "Yes, but ..." No *but* required! Sometimes we have to lean forward and take one step at a time!

"When should we start leaning forward?" you may ask. I recommend starting as soon as possible (i.e., now). I advise that if you foresee an issue, plan for it now and be prepared to adjust depending on the situation. Abraham Lincoln once said, "Give me six hours to chop down a tree and I will spend the first four sharpening the axe."

Many successful people are successful because of the planning and work that the masses do not see. Do you think Michael Jordan, Babe Ruth, Wayne Gretzky, Walter Payton, Usain Bolt, Martin Luther King Jr., Mother Teresa, Theodore Roosevelt, Barack Obama, and many other leaders of great nations, but most important of all, you are where you are by not studying, learning, rehearsing, and practicing? I think not!

At least for me, that's going to be a no. Can you start at any time? Yes! There is no better time than the present! Start where you are with what you have! The earlier you start, the greater the ability to avoid unexpected changes toward the end.

I'm not telling you to go out and look for or make things rough on yourself. All I'm saying is when life gives you lemons, step back to evaluate the situation, pour tequila shots, slice that lemon, and take that shit to the head and call for another round. I think of a scene from *Forrest Gump*. During a rainstorm, Lieutenant Dan grabbed hold of the ship and welcomed the hell he was in. He even called out to God, all while the other shrimp boats had docked and feared the storm.

Again, he took his shots and said "fuck it!" His "fuck it" (persistence) found him the only functioning shrimping boat in the area, resulting in the creation of Bubba Gump Shrimp Company. What if he had given up? Would he have gotten legs, or could Forrest have afforded to take care of Jenny, his mom, or Bubba's mom? Think about that for a minute. Understand the desired end state of Lieutenant Dan and Forrest Gump.

According to Dictionary.com a is trial, a noun, is defined as:

1. the examination before a judicial tribunal of the facts put in issue in a cause, often including issues of law as well as those of fact.

2. the determination of a person's guilt or innocence by due process of law the act of trying, testing, or putting to the proof.

3. An attempt or effort to do something.

A tribulation, a noun, is defined as "grievous trouble; severe." (Dictionary.com)

Trials and tribulations help us build that courage needed to make it to the finish line. A trial is exactly that. Let's look at it from another perspective. The first example is that which is received in the mail or seen on TV or social media feeds. If you don't like the product at a specific time, it can be returned of course, normally at no charge.

The second example involves court proceedings. In court, you have a defendant accused of a crime. The purpose of this type of trial is to present evidence in a systematic process in order to persuade the judge and/or jury to prosecute or acquit the accused. Both instances require a subject or person endure some type of situation. However, pressing to the end is the only way to get to the desired end state.

What type of person are you? Do you think differently than those you work with? Do you strive to be the best in everything you do? Do you feel it is important that you do what you feel is right regardless of what others may think? Do you project positivity onto your environment whether through a smile, greeting, or your presence in general?

If you answer yes to any of those questions, you are on the road to success. Wait! Wait! Wait! Don't shut down if you didn't. You're reading this book. That means you now have the blueprint to that road. Let's kill it together. You are not alone. I too once found myself conforming to my environment and not it to me. I finally realized that success was subjective and the only person to define my success was me.

That's right! I am the captain of my own ship! I learned what made me happy and how to focus on what my heart desired. Yes, I lost some people, for instance, friends, family, jobs, and opportunities. However, what I opened was Pandora's box—from the new friends (who are now family) to stronger family bonds and opportunities I can't even begin to express or keep up with the magnitude of prospects I was presented with, from being the COO of an amazing security company to a real-life superhero for my son and countless other artists looking to sculpt their bodies and minds.

However, if I would not have been persistent in evaluating the 5W's, I would have been lost up Shit's Creek without a paddle or boat. Thank God! My "fuck it" kicked in, and that stubbornness within me refused to let me conform. What's in you? Come on! Dig deep! That voice telling you to keep pushing is right. Get up! Don't you quit! Look who is depending on your success! Who is it? What's your reason why? If you have forgotten, refer back to the first chapter's exercise.

I will now paint a picture of what persistence is using three familiar stories. During these stories, try to think of when you were in a similar predicament and how persistence, or lack of, played a part in your success or failure.

Story 1

The first is about a man who was raised by a family of different ethnic origin but was considered family (half-son and half-brother). This is one of the greatest Bible stories of all time. If you haven't guessed already, this is the story of Moses and the Israelites. The story goes that Moses was found as a baby and raised with the royal family. He knew he was different and felt it in his heart. His Egyptian stepmother told him his ethnicity (Hebrew), which compelled him to see how his people were enslaved, and it vexed him greatly.

God came to him and told him to go to Pharaoh (his half-brother) and tell him to let God's people go! Moses did so and was denied and ridiculed for doing so. This enraged Pharaoh, which caused him to inflict discomfort on the Hebrews. This happened seven times, and six out of seven times, Pharaoh cursed God and Moses.

God told Moses of the plagues prior to inflicting them on the Egyptians. Since the Egyptians raised Moses, it hurt him to see the suffering of the people, but he had to maintain pressure and be persistent in his task to free God's people and steward them to the Promised Land. There came a point when Moses was at the Red Sea and Pharaoh's army was in hot pursuit, intending to kill and destroy the Hebrews. This caused frustration and discord amongst the masses, but Moses stayed focused (i.e., trusted and believed in the word of God) that he would lead the people to the Promised Land.

This is where most people would have had major anxiety attacks (and rightfully so). Moses raised his staff and parted the Red Sea, allowing people to cross on dry land. Do you know how much persistence it takes to overcome the life-threatening fears one after the other? Wow! What thoughts would you have going through your mind? Would you still have pressed on?

Story 2

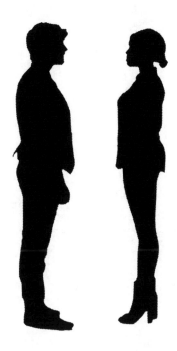

The second story is about a young man named Tony. He was married at the age of twenty-one and joined the military to provide for his family. However, after the first year, he knew this wasn't the right wife for him, but he did not believe in divorce, as most of us don't. So he suffered daily with working long days, just to go home to a messy house and not a home-cooked meal in sight unless the Food Network was on. This resulted in constant arguments.

For seven years, this went on. Tony, a kindhearted individual, didn't want to see his wife's three brothers in foster homes and told her they should adopt them. Now she worked various jobs on and off when Tony complained or when she was trying to run a Ponzi scheme on someone. So two of the three brothers came to live with them. Tony's wife said the other one was too much.

Tony had been deployed to Iraq twice before, and before each, his wife had told him during arguments, "I hope you die!" As you may have figured out, his wife is a money-hungry, gold-digging bitch. She only wanted the military benefits she could get and the $400,000 life insurance payout if he died, since she was the beneficiary. Additionally she got money for her brothers, which he never found out about until after their divorce. Why didn't she help with the bills? It's just a thought.

Tony was scheduled to deploy to Afghanistan in February, but in December he found out that the money she was given to pay the mortgage and other bills had not been used for that purpose. They then agreed to separate. During the separation, Tony's wife called his chain of command and reported that he was cheating on her with a lower enlisted soldier. Tony was in a club with his friend, Quinn, whom his wife knew.

Tony's first sergeant called him while he was in the club on Quinn's phone and told him to come in the next day. He also put him on a seventy-two-hour no-contact order. Now, isn't that some bullshit? That meant he couldn't go to his house where he paid for everything, the true definition of fuckery.

After this incident, Tony was taken off deployment and forced to counseling. Then one bright shiny day, five days before the deployment, Tony went home to his wife's middle brother, Jacob, who asked to speak to him outside.

When they got outside, Jacob told Tony that he had heard his sister on the phone talking to her grandmother, saying how she was going to run off with she and Tony's newborn son and how she had stolen money (e.g., mortgage and bills).

Four days later, she did. She put the house ten months behind, stole a large amount of money, and told people that Tony had physically assaulted her, which was found to be false. On the day she left, he was at work with witnesses, but he had been calling home all day with no response.

Then finally at six o'clock, he got a dinner break and went home to find the house looking like there had been a struggle and the people in the house had been taken. But why were all the baby items missing?

Tony instantly called the police, who were very unhelpful. As they walked across the street to talk to a neighbor, he then came back and told them she had left with a baby. Thank you, Captain Obvious! Tony sat in the middle of the living room floor and cried. Yup! A grown-ass man cried. He didn't know what to do but wait there more! His wife had run off with the child, stolen money, created an enormous debt, filed for child support, and continued to try to affect his career. She even had the audacity to request spousal support.

However, Tony had a thought that one of his old friends used to say, "I like being at rock bottom because there's nowhere to go but up." Although Tony didn't agree with liking being at rock bottom, he understood the significance of that statement. At that moment, he knew that life posed greater things for him. He got up, cleaned up, and went back to work to finish his shift and outline the problem he faced.

Using the 5Ws, Tony was able to see clearly what he needed to do. He had massive debt, a house entering foreclosure, a missing child, and a military career now in jeopardy. His window to reenlist was open at the time, and he was thinking of getting out. Now his circumstances had changed. He decided to reenlist for the bonus, to earn some money to eliminate some debt.

He deployed the following January, where he earned deployment wages and was able to continue to pay off debt. It took about ten years to crawl out of the hole, but at the end of the tunnel, the light shines bright. Tony's only debt is a mortgage that is now current. His persistence empowers him with a well-organized business mindset, a consistent cash flow, and more assets than liabilities.

Tony now owns multiple properties and several cars. As far as his stability, let's just say he doesn't worry about not having enough money for something. The 5Ws worked perfectly for him. Although he continues to fight for custody of his son, he does see him. Tony is retiring from the military and remains debt-free. He now helps others build wealth for themselves and future generations. Can you think of a time in your life when you could have benefited from this knowledge?

Story 3

This story takes place in a foreign land. In 2010, I was in Dubai, working in a special section for the military. One day a coworker asked if anyone had talked to me about moving back to my original section. I informed him that I had not and would engage the supervisor about it.

When I talked to the supervisor, he said that because we were both preparing to redeploy, it was in the best interest to realign our forces, which made a lot of sense to me, and it would be effective on Monday or Tuesday.

On Sunday, something happened, and I was being lied about, which caused a large investigation. This had a ripple effect, causing administration action to be imposed and flagged, a notification for anyone looking at a person's file, informing them that the person is restricted from certain liberties such as being recommended for awards, promotions, schools, and even certain jobs.

This bothered me immensely, but I knew I had done nothing wrong until I was told I was a suspect in a crime I didn't commit. In my previous experience as a senior enlisted soldier, I knew it would be in my best interest to not waive my rights and request a lawyer. This seemed to upset a lot of people, including my chain of command and the military police. However, it was the right thing to do. So like Nike says, "Just do it!" I did.

Once I did, higher headquarters decided to push it to the lower level to possibly avoid publicly and possibly discrediting senior officers and enlisted personnel. When my unit took control of it, they blew it out of control. They began to focus their efforts on trying to frame me for something. I mean, they accused me of several things: being AWOL, using a nontactical vehicle, illegally possessing alcohol, being off post by myself, and not having written approval to go off base. So let's break down each allegation so you can get a better picture of how I was not guilty.

Being AWOL

AWOL is defined as being unaccounted for due to missing some type of meeting that must have been known and not being seen or heard from in eighteen hours. But when I called my supervisor to ask how I was AWOL, he said I was unaccountable for fourteen and a half hours. Now what stands out here? Time! Fourteen and a half hours does not equal eighteen hours. Maybe it's the new math the kids are learning nowadays!

Using a Nontactical Vehicle

To use a nontactical vehicle in another country, you must be licensed and dispatched a vehicle. I was not driving because I did not have a license. Wow! You would think they would stop there, but oh no!

Illegally Possessing Alcohol

Dubai is a dry country, and it's illegal to have alcohol. Additionally, because I was deployed, the military prohibits it, making it fall under what is referred to as "General Order No. 1." When my two coworkers were searching, doing a routine inspection, a water bottle filled with gin was found. However, I had not been in the truck for several hours and could not account for who was in the truck before me or what had transpired between the time I had separated from the truck and the search. There was at least a six-hour gap.

So I was not in the vehicle at the time of seizure? My eyebrow was raised! Tell me again: how do I have possession? Don't worry. I'll wait. Regardless if one or maybe even both guys try to blame me for the alcohol, the word *possession* refutes that argument completely. The word *possession* itself encompasses time and space to be centrally located.

So if I'm not in the truck but miles away, how do I have possession? If that's true, then I must be responsible for the actions of every person on earth. I remember a commercial that used to say, "Inquiring minds would like to know." Damn it, I am one of those inquiring minds! But I digress.

Not Having Written Approval to Go Off Base

The two-man rule states that you have to be with someone with the proper ID card off base. However, the only way for them to determine if you were off base by yourself is when you return, that is, if you're alone or not. If you come back by yourself, then you are in violation. In my situation, I was with a buddy who had the appropriate ID. I was going to hang with him anyway.

He was going to bring me back to base after all of his errands were done. That was until I had to get back sooner due to receiving an anonymous call saying that my unit was saying I was AWOL. This information caused me to get a ride back by calling my unit to come pick me up because the person's car would not be finished for another hour.

Once I came back, I made the appropriate contact with leadership and the military police. As you can see, I was never by myself, and because they were not with me, they cannot prove otherwise. Now what do you would think would be the final allegation? Of course, the off-post memo approval.

As I came from Iraq, I had no knowledge of needing written approval. Only getting a battle buddy and vehicle were the norm. The last general directive said it would be on the unit to make written approval needed necessary at the battalion and brigade levels, which had not been done. This happened even in the presence of leadership, and the last email I had seen about his stated written approval was no longer needed. Besides, you can't just single out one person for what the entire unit and base are doing! How is this fair? It sounds like a complaint to me!

On top of that, three months prior, I was sent a package that contained alcohol. The funny thing is that it was sent to an address where I did not receive mail. Hold your judgment a little while longer, please. Someone unknown to me sent the package. Additionally, Customs confiscated the box before I received it and sent me a letter. I was confused because I didn't know the person, but I was expecting a box containing protein and preworkout, which came later through my unit.

Customs sent me a letter detailing what was in the box. I displayed the letter around the office, as I did not know who it was from. Nor did I ask anyone for it, so I didn't think much of it after that until three months later after the investigating officer talked to the MPs and they decided to open an investigation on me for that. Stupid, right?

My command submitted for a suspension of my top-secret clearance. "But why?" you may ask. That's a good question, and I wish I knew the answer to tell you. But what I can tell you is that I asked for the reason and he was very childish about it. He told me he was given information and sent me a regulation that further supported what I'd been saying the entire time.

As I read the regulation, I found that he was supposed to tell me in detail, via a written format. So why did he refuse? One reason is because his justification was that I was drinking and receiving alcohol. So during this entire story when I had a drink and I never received any unless I was Customs, so now he lied on an official document. SMH!

It's like they say. If you give someone enough rope, they will hang themselves. My God, that's what they did by trying to frame me. Sadly, I must go through all this to prove my innocence. I had to get the Inspector General and Equal Opportunity involved. Now by doing so, I understand I may get blackballed in the military, but it ensures the toxic leadership that corrupts the unit is removed and numerous others will have a better life because of it. It's worth it because at this point, I've been in for seventeen and a half years and it could all go away without retirement if I'm blackballed. Now you tell me if that's sacrifice or what?

I firmly believe it is better to give than receive, although sometimes it may get rough. I shall not be moved! In times like the previous descriptions, I can hear one of the major generals that I know telling me it is never as bad as it seems! What's your story?

Exercise

1. Write a positive quote and place it somewhere you can see it often several times a day. Choose something that gets you fired up!

2. Analyze every situation and pick out the positive aspects as a result of the outcome, for example, a right-handed basketball player breaking their right hand but becoming better with their left as the right heals.

3. Make a list consisting of what is desired for the month, week, and day; why it is desired; when you want to achieve this goal; where you are now in the progression of achievement; and how you plan to get from start to finish, executing tasks from your plan daily for twenty-one days.

Chapter 3

SACRIFICE

John Wooden once said, "Things work out best for those who make the best of how things work out."

What exactly is sacrifice? I mean a true sacrifice! I'm talking about going without heat in Chicago's winter to buy Christmas gifts for children who still believe in Santa Claus or simply giving up any need to be put in a better position to achieve a desire. According to scholars and Dictionary.com, sacrifice is a noun, meaning the offering of animal, plant, or human life or of some material possession to a deity, as in propitiation or homage; the person, animal, or thing so offered; the render or destruction of something price or desirable for the sake of something considered as having a higher or more pressing claim.

Amazing, right? So how much would you sacrifice? You may have asked this question yourself. The answer is—are you ready for it—yes! I know, but to achieve any goal is all subjective to how much each person desires that achievement.

For example, some people gamble all the time (e.g., casinos, horse tracks, sporting events, etc.). Some win, and others lose, but a pattern for a majority of the winners and losers is that they took a big risk and sacrificed a large sum, which would result in a big win or loss.

Let's look at the other side of the law. Let me put this disclaimer out there that I hate drugs unless they are in the use of healing someone. Drug cartels risk their life so they may have big success, at least what they deem to be a success, but when caught or killed, it's a big loss. Military servicepeople, when deciding to fight an armed enemy or break contact due to unfavorable odds (i.e., kill or be killed) will result in victory or defeat. But as the U.S. military, all we do is win, fight, win!

So ask yourself: how much am I willing to put on the line for your desires, dreams, goals, and/or visions? Remember, fear has a larger body count than any disease you can think of, even if all were combined.

So what does your heart desire? Obtaining it is worth how much to you? During an old commercial, they would sing, "What would you do for a Klondike bar [an ice cream bar]?" In the commercial, there would be people fighting polar bears and doing the most unbelievable things for a Klondike bar.

If ice cream can generate such a great sacrifice, I can't even begin to scratch the surface of what you are capable of in obtaining your heart's desire. Forget an arm and a leg. You might be giving up your firstborn! No, but seriously what is it worth to you? Is it worth your all or just a little bit of you? Have you heard the saying, "You get out of something what you put into it"? It is truly better to give than receive, meaning when you give, it comes back a greater blessing. So basically you are setting the conditions for a brighter future win!

Story 1

In the Bible, there is a story of a man, Abraham, and his son, Isaac. He believed God would provide for his every need. One day, God told him to go to the land of Moriah and offer up his firstborn, whom he loved so much, as a burnt offering. This troubled Abraham, but he trusted God. So the following day, Abraham, Isaac, and two other young men went up to the mountain. Once they got to the mountain, they prepared the wood for the offering on the third day. Abraham told the two young men to wait with the donkey as he and Isaac would go to the designated place and worship God.

When they got to the destination, wood was laid upon Isaac with troubled Abraham standing with knife in hand. Isaac then asked his father where the lamb was for offering, as he was unwittingly the proposed lamb. Abraham told Isaac that God would provide the lamb. Isaac was then laid on the altar, and Abraham began the action of taking his son's life.

At that moment, an angel stopped him. God spoke to him again, saying not to harm Isaac. He proceeded to tell him that now he knows how much he fears God and to sacrifice a ram in the bush. Wow! Now that that's putting it all on the line. Imagine having to kill or give up what you love the most. Could you do it? Yes, absolutely you can! Let's look at another story.

Story 2

The Bible highlights in John 3:16, in my opinion, the most significant sacrifice man has ever known since existence. It states that God loved the world (i.e., man) so much that he gave his only son, whom he also loved, to the world, knowing they would torture and kill his body to gain the overall result of saving the world from evil.

However, the COVID-19 pandemic has definitely created a multitude of people who made sacrifices for their fellow man, such as doctors, servicepeople, law-abiding police, grocery store and fast-food workers, individuals who work in the logistics field as a whole, and many more. All the sacrifices made, either biblical or currently, was to achieve the greater good for man in the long run. What's your story?

Exercise

This week's exercise will focus on sacrifice. It is better to give than to receive because of the greater gain at the end. So this week, I want you to look at the plan you created in the second chapter. Look at the requirement and what you have given up for it. You have given something up for your dreams to become closer to a reality. It doesn't have to be something big, but it must be something that can have a huge culminating effect. In the words of Alexander Stroddard "What we do today, right now, will have an accumulated effect on all our tomorrow's!" (https://www.passiton.com/inspirational-quotes/6172-what-we-do-today-rig)

"Just do it" for one week, or maybe two, and if you like the results and feel motivated, continue until you reach your heart's desire.

In this chapter, we defined what sacrifice is, how much, and when you should. We also stated that we must make sure the juice is worth the squeeze. The two stories included highlight sacrifice, both biblical and personal. With all these nuggets, you have the knowledge and power to accomplish an exceptional future. Now go! Sacrifice awaits you!

Chapter 4

SUCCESS

In this chapter, we will define what success is, understand why it is important, take a deep dive into why celebrating with others is a part of being successful, and how the law of attraction plays a part of every success.

Success is defined as the favorable or prosperous termination of attempts or endeavors, the accomplishment of our goals. There are other definitions, but they all result in the attainment of goals. Because we all have different goals, our determination of what success is to us is unique to each individual. So again, what is your heart's desire? Do you have a road map for achieving it? What are you willing to go through for it, and what sacrifices are you going to make?

Many people think success is important because one can become rich, famous, or a part of a certain social group. All of that may be true, but being successful has other perks as well. When becoming successful, very few jump from the bottom to the top by skipping the trials and tribulations in between. Although we like to be able to quote Drake, the hip-hop artist, saying, "I started from the bottom! Now I'm here!" success is something that starts with the smallest progression toward a goal, for instance, passing a class in working to obtain an associate's, bachelor's, master's, or doctorate.

In this sense, a person can become motivated to take the next class or enroll in an additional class to speed up their progression in the process. Either way, through small successes or wins, as some may call them, they generate a positive attitude, which projects on everything that's done afterward as long as that hunger to succeed last. Will it go away? Absolutely! If it is not fed with more small wins, it will die, but this ties into the law of attraction.

Do you think success is important? Why or why not? Just think of the feeling you get when you obtain a small and big win. It feels great, right? But would you have been able to have that larger win if there were no small wins, for instance, one touchdown versus winning the whole game. My guess is no!

To build a house, you must first build a strong foundation and build from the bottom to the top, not top-down. It's one brick at a time. Think about that for a moment. How are you trying to reach your heart's desire? Are you gradually elevating or making large jumps? Statistically speaking, large jumps don't work and eventually result in going back to the beginning, the starting point of one's endeavors. In other words, we are going nowhere fast.

When we achieve success, we must celebrate with others. Yes, it is good to celebrate alone first, for instance, dance when no one is looking, scream, jump for joy, or even take yourself out for dinner, drinks, or whatever else excites you. Why do we have to involve others in something we did? Truth be told, there is nothing on this earth that we did solely alone.

Just think about it. Whether it was advice, some sort of counseling, an invention that made things we used, or, in my opinion, God, we had assistance! So why not allow those who are cheering for us to feel happy or like they were valuable to us? We're not that selfish, and it shows by our ability to be successful. We both know at times you want to quit, but we thought about how it would affect others or be viewed by someone else.

Celebrating with others builds a stronger bond as well as facilitates a positive environment. So let the good times flow! Enjoy your win and give others the motivation to push closer to their goals. You are the one. You can make it happen by sharing. After all, sharing is caring! Don't be fooled. Not everyone on your team is cheering for you. So for those people (AKA haters), I like to remember Frank Sinatra's quote, "The best revenge is massive success!"

They want you to fail, to give up, to just stop being persistent. Haters would love to see your goals, visions, and dreams suffer from a heart attack. Well, it is not theirs to determine. Turn the table and kill them by proving them wrong and having a healthy heart (heart's desire). If you want to know who they are, look at the faces during each of your achievements, and if they look like they smell shit and they can't stand you, bring them a chair because they are in for a long exhibition.

The law of attraction is very real. Whatever you put out is going to come back even greater. That's just how it works! An apple tree can only bear apples, and we can only receive what we project out.

Story 1

An African-American girl was born in Kosciusko, Mississippi, in 1954. This girl's childhood was not one of doll houses and tea parties. It was more of home instability, sexual abuse, and strictness. However, she pressed through the different times and received a top-notch education in Tennessee at home and an institutional education. The young lady's focus landed her on radio, TV, and even in the White House. If you haven't guessed it, it's one of the most successful women in the world, Oprah Gail Winfrey. She is one of the highest-paid entertainers in the globe, going from a farm in Mississippi to a mansion in Chicago. Now talk about rags to riches!

Story 2

The second story truly tested this man's faith. He displayed the true definition of persistence. Although he lived during biblical times, God blessed him. As the story goes, he and his family lived a comfortable life until the devil (AKA haters) intervened in hopes of killing his dreams, goals, and desires. Now that's the boss of all haters, so he can use all the people and things to inflict his plan to destroy dreams. His victim was stripped of his good health, respect from family and friends, his wife's encouragement (telling him to curse his God and die), and having all his materialistic things stripped from him. It brought his social status to an all-time low, but he didn't give in to peer pressure and knew God was good. He realized that God had allowed his current situation to exist. Who is he? That's right! Job!

There was no way I could write this book on persistence and not talk about Job. He refused all attempts to lure him in to give up on God. See, this made God proud he blessed Job tenfold. Just think if Job had $1,000,000, he was blessed ten times with every aspect in his life. Now who could deny that was a success (big win)? Job followed the road map that we have drawn in this book. First and foremost, he had a goal to honor and have faith in God. He was persistent, and he never gave in, regardless of the negativity that he faced. Finally he made the necessary sacrifices, including losing children, friends, and the things we as human value the most.

Story 3

The final story of the book is now upon you. This is about Frederick Douglass. He was born a slave. Douglass endured slavery, as what was referred to as a house nigger, as a child. His master's wife taught him letters and how to read until her husband found out. The master forbid his wife from teaching Frederick anymore. Being the persistent young man Frederick was, he figured out ways to continue his learning. He would give bread to others in exchange for the poor white kids on his way to and from the market for lessons. Frederick would also copy letters and words from books around the house and practice them with the assistance of the poor white kids. Before long, he taught himself to read and write, which was unheard of for a slave or anyone else during that time. He told no one as he would have surely been punished.

Frederick later wrote his own freedom papers and escaped from slavery. He later became an activist and author, amongst many other talents he developed over time. Nowadays, if it is not in a game format, children don't want to have anything to do with it. However, here was a child going through so much who still formulated a dream. He found ways to accomplish the dream through all the adversity, as well as make the sacrifices that would have caused most of us to have PTSD, at a minimum, but persistence prevailed.

What's your story?

Epilogue

Now take the lessons of this book and not only live your best life but love your best life. We have seen and experienced a time when we had a heart's desire (vision, dream, or goal) just to let it never come true due to one of the three types of CVDs. We made the correlation of the physical heart and the emotional heart to emphasize the importance of life to your desires are to one's existence. Having a heart's desire or whatever is appropriate for you to call it has always been a key element in a productive and successful life. Individuals have figured it out, as biblical and modern stories have proven.

Sometimes we have to take a risk and be persistent in life. This discipline could very well be the deciding factor of a person's entire life. As Mr. Hill stated, we could be three feet from gold. Each person has to find that "fuck it" within themselves and pursue their goals. There is no point in stopping once you have entered the storm, so it would only be wise to get that pot of gold at the end of the rainbow. Plus lemons are multipurpose fruits, depending on your persistence.

Regardless of what we want in life, a sacrifice is necessary. The greater the goal, the greater the sacrifice. Sometimes we have to put it all on the line, like Abraham or essential workers during COVID-19, to obtain a greater reward. This too has been tested and proven throughout the pages of history.

Some things are designed to be (with the right formula). Success begins the ultimate end game of all endeavors. By following the road map of defining one's heart desire, being persistent about obtaining the desire and making the necessary sacrifices along the way will guarantee success in any arena.

So I pose the question again: what is success to you?

About the Author

Alstria Lavar Compton was born September 8, 1980, to Charlene Compton of Chicago, Illinois. He is a highly decorated soldier with two tours to Afghanistan and three tours to Iraq, where he earned three Meritorious Unit Citations, one Joint Meritorious Unit Citation, one Bronze Star, two Joint Commendation Medals, two Army Commendation Medals, one Army Achievement Medal, Iraqi Campaign Service Medal, Afghanistan Campaign

Service Medal, Global War on Terrorism Expeditionary Medal, and Combat Action Badge, amongst many other stateside awards such as three Meritorious Service Medals.

Compton's focus of studies is psychology, leadership, fitness, and economics. Currently he has served on active duty for the past eighteen and a half years. He has been one of the most persistent individuals to grace the earth. This is evident in his climb from being homeless to higher middle class, the point where you have a little more than milk money. He is a small business owner, personal trainer, and life coach. His passion to help others find the way to success has been a driving force throughout his life. His goal is to have a positive impact on everyone possible and make the world a better place.

Compton's reason for this book is to assist in stimulating others' ability to think outside of their current thoughts and develop a road map to each person's personal success and prepare for the struggle, but know there is a pot of gold at the end of the rainbow if one puts in the effort and stays. Persistent success is right beyond the struggle.

Printed in the United States
by Baker & Taylor Publisher Services